The Sacrament of Confession

The
Sacrament *of*
Confession

What It Is *and*
How to Receive It Well

Very Reverend Canon
Héctor R.G. Pérez,
S.T.D., C.S.L.J.

SOPHIA INSTITUTE PRESS
Manchester, New Hampshire

Sophia Institute Press
Box 5284, Manchester, NH 03108
1-800-888-9344
www.SophiaInstitute.com

Sophia Institute Press® is a registered trademark of Sophia Institute.

Imprimatur and *nihil obstat*: Most Rev. William A. Wack D.D., C.S.C.
January 31, 2019

paperback ISBN 978-1-64413-782-6

ebook ISBN 978-1-64413-783-3

Library of Congress Control Number: 2022941832

First printing

To Our Lady of Laus

Contents

The Sacrament of Confession

Introduction

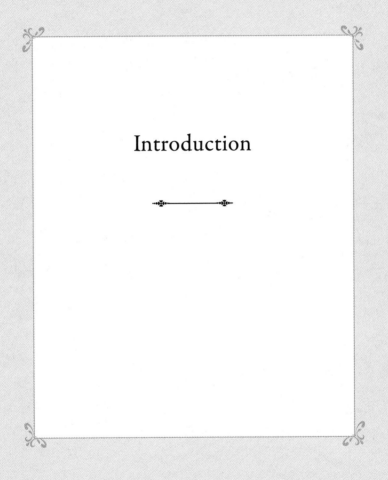

We have been taught in our catechism that the seven sacraments are the principal channels of God's grace to us His children in His Mystical Body, the Church. Among these seven sacraments, there are three that have a privilege and peculiarity in themselves. They are, indeed, very special because they give life, or restore life, to those who are spiritually dead (CCC 1420–1421). They are dead because of serious sin, whether original sin or actual mortal sin. As we read in the Psalms: "in sin my mother conceived me" (51:7). Each of us, then, without exception, is born with the death sentence of original sin committed by our first parents, Adam and Eve. This sin is handed down by generations—from our first parents to the end of time—in the blood, which we receive in our mother's womb from the moment of our conception. Thus, we are born to life spiritually dead. As such, we have need, an absolute need, of that sacrament that Christ has instituted to wash us of original sin; to restore us to friendship to Himself; to give us the life of the very Trinity into our souls, that is, the life of sanctifying grace; to give us the "power to become children of God" (John 1:12); to make us members, thus of His Family, which on earth is the one, holy, catholic, and apostolic Church. All this is accomplished by this one sacrament— this excellent channel of God's grace.

Now, as each of us can testify, there is more to the story. The Sacrament of Baptism, as wonderful and necessary as it is, does not do away with all the effects of original sin: the curse of illness, aging, and death; the necessity to work "from the sweat of our brow" (see Gen. 3:17–19) to earn our livelihood; pain at childbirth; among others. These remain. They do not go away with the cleansing waters of Baptism. In addition, perhaps among the worst effects of original sin, something else remains in us. Baptism does not take away from us the *fomes peccati*—the curse of concupiscence. This means that as green plants tend toward the sun or any type of light, we human beings tend toward sin and every type of evil. (This can be verified even in babies and little, otherwise innocent, children.) We face a real challenge, a real conundrum. But God is all-wise, all-knowing. He would not lead us to life just to drop us like a lead balloon. He has provided us with the means to reach eternal life, despite all our defects.

Among the means provided by the all-merciful God, in His Church and in the economy of salvation that He has set up for us, again, are the three sacraments which are called the sacraments of the dead: Baptism, Unction or Anointing, and Penance or Confession. Through Baptism we are cleansed of original sin and brought to life, the life of the Trinity, grace. In Holy Unction, or Anointing, those who are seriously ill or dying (especially unconscious, as those who are aware would have to confess their sins) may be anointed and receive both spiritual pardon and, sometimes, healing of their ailments—thus it brings us back doubly from death to life. Through the Sacrament of Penance, or Confession, a person may confess his or her sins, whether venial or mortal, to a priest and after expressing sorrow and a desire to amend the way of life, receive absolution and forgiveness, thus coming back to life. This is why these three sacraments are known as the sacraments of the dead. Our God is so kind and considerate of us and our nature, with all its foibles, that He has not left a stone unturned to make sure we are afforded every means of salvation! It is this last sacrament that we wish to deal with here.

It seems that many persons have problems or difficulties when it comes to Confession. I, on the other hand, consider it one of my favorite sacraments (after Holy Communion). Along with Communion it can be received as frequently

The Sacrament of Confession

as necessary and possible—even daily. Spiritually speaking, Confession is like taking a hot shower. How good it is to be washed clean of sweat, dirt, and grime! How good it feels for our tired and aching bodies, our muscles and joints, to be cleansed under the rejuvenating flow of the hot water! For the soul of one who wants to continue, or return, to the fullness of friendship with God, Confession is just such a cleansing!

Now, I realize that as much as I like this Sacrament of Confession and enjoy its fruits, for the majority of Catholics, the prospect of confessing our sins—our deepest and darkest secrets and actions that make us feel embarrassed or ashamed, our most hidden thoughts—to the priest is oftentimes a paralyzing thing. This also often keeps converts, at least for a time, or perhaps always, from fully entering into the full communion of the Church. Even many so-called cradle-born Catholics find some level of difficulty in this. How sad! (Now we will not go into some of the reasons for this, including poor catechesis or the rare, but scary, encounter with a priest who, instead of reconciling sinners, chases them away. In the old days, not every priest was allowed to hear Confessions. In my own training at the Vatican, we were both trained and tested before we could hear Confessions. Alas, this is not done in too many places today. A good confessor, while being strict, is also merciful, kind, and affable to those who humble themselves in the tribunal of the confessional. But this is not a seminary class.) Again, many of us have run into a priest who was mean and unkind to us in the confessional. Not only is this not the ideal situation but also that particular confessor needs a lot of prayers. Only God knows what is in his heart and his past that may have prompted such behavior. Needless to say, I do not condone it at all. Luckily, for the most part, most confessors are kind and loving—and hopefully strict enough to get us right back on the right path. But they admonish us always with charity and kindness. As a result, we must try to rid ourselves of any fears we may have about Confession. We must realize it is a good thing to be had, to be made.

In keeping away from Confession, a person foregoes a necessary means of salvation and healing. Ven. Archbishop Fulton J. Sheen would decry the millions of dollars spent by people on psychologists when a good, thorough Confession would have been more efficacious. And free!

Confession, in fact, is necessary for each and every one of us. While the Church does teach that one can make an act of perfect contrition and be forgiven, especially in emergencies, it is only realistic to realize that this is almost impossible. Why? To make an act of perfect contrition requires that our motives be totally pure. It means that we are *only* concerned with the fact that by sinning we have offended God. That is to be our only motive. Alas, we are made of complicated elements, so to speak. Our Lord well knew this in giving us this wonderful sacrament.

We seldom have pure motives. What does this mean? It means we are concerned with: shame of our sin; fear of being found out by others; we fear that God will punish us in this life; we fear being cast into the eternal fires of Hell; and other motives. All these make our contrition imperfect, what traditional theology calls "attrition" — it is contrition mixed in with some or all of the above. As such, the Sacrament of Penance makes perfect that which in us is imperfect. This, then, grants us forgiveness as long as we have the intentions of being truly sorry for our sins; to make reparation or penance according to what the priest tells us but also additional forms of private penance which we can do ourselves; and a true and sincere desire and purpose of amendment, i.e., we will strive with the help of God to avoid this or these sins in the future. Needless to say, if we have no intention of avoiding a particular sin or occasion of sin, then we can obtain no pardon — even if the confessor, in his human ignorance, does not know the true intentions of the one confessing.

Another question that often comes up is that of mortal sin versus venial sin. Venial sin does not kill the life of grace in our souls. A multiplicity of them, especially unrepented and unconfessed, however, does weaken the soul, enabling it to more readily fall into deadly, or mortal, sin. Thus, while we have no strict obligation to confess venial sins, it is much more salutary for us to do so—and often. (If one wants to obtain a plenary indulgence for any act, Confession is required within eight days of said act, thus not confessing frequently also deprives us of the possibility of obtaining plenary indulgences.) St. Thomas Aquinas mentions that confessing venial sins lessens our time in Purgatory. That seems to be more than enough reason to receive the Sacrament.

What can we say about mortal sin? It destroys the life of God, the life of sanctifying grace, within our souls! It is tantamount to us telling God to get out of our souls and slamming the door in His face! One cannot merit or obtain any grace or indulgence while in mortal sin. One must not receive any sacrament. Any sacrament thus received is nullified. In the case of Confirmation and Holy Matrimony, the sacrament remains in limbo, so to speak, until Confession takes place. (Once we have confessed, the sacrament may come alive and grow within us as intended.) But it is also a mortal sin of sacrilege to receive any sacrament in the state of mortal sin. It multiplies itself with interest. That means that we ought to confess any and all mortal sins as soon as possible. In the meantime, if no priest is available, then we should say as perfect an act of contrition as possible. But since we have attrition (i.e., imperfect contrition) 99 percent of the time, we should not relax until we have fully confessed our sins. Thus, Confession is not just a pretty thing or object that we can or cannot have. It is not like another unnecessary knickknack on our mantelpiece or an ornament on our Christmas tree. According to the economy of salvation set up by God Himself, it is most necessary, indeed.

The Confession Itself

Now we can pay attention to the practicalities of going to Confession. One of my friends tells of an old Jesuit priest who related to him that there are three Bs to Confession: Be brutal, Be brief, and Be gone! Many people think Confession is a session on spiritual direction. While most people cannot have the luxury of a spiritual director (who are rare in this age), we cannot hold up the line with all our non-essential problems. Confession is also not a psychologist's couch. While some priests have extensive psychological training, most don't. Do not burden him or endanger him into being wrong.

When we enter the confessional, kneel (or sit)—a confessional with a kneeler and a screen for privacy and protection for the priest is preferred and mandated by law (Canon 964: 2-3 in the 1983 Code of Canon Law), even if so-called "face-to-face Confessions" are allowed. (In the present state of affairs and environment, I would not recommend face-to-face Confessions at all as there are far too many dangers for confessors.) Begin by saying "Forgive me, Father, for I have sinned." The custom of saying "Bless me" is very unusual and only found in America. It makes no sense. But it is not a sin to say that, though I prefer the above. Then, unless the priest is very familiar with us and knows who we are, we should say: "I am a single man/woman"; "I am a married man/woman"; or "I am a priest/bishop." In other words, we tell the priest our station in life. This will help him know the seriousness of any of our sins as well as the proper advice and penance to give. Then we should list our sins simply without making any excuses for ourselves, such as: "I have taken the name of the Lord in vain"; "I have committed this or that sin of impurity"; "I have destroyed another's reputation with gossip or calumny"; "I have missed Mass on Sunday/a holy day"; "I have received Communion in the state of mortal sin." You should not say something like: "Someone made me really angry and made me take the name of God in vain."

One of the problems confessors often run into is that many try to confess another person's sins rather than their own, such as: "My husband/wife did this" or "My sister/brother took this from me." So many give excuses and reasons to try to alleviate their own guilt and responsibility. If we know someone else did wrong, then we should advise them of it. It is a spiritual work of mercy to admonish the sinner and advise those in error. We should not try to confess their sins. We should only concentrate on our own sins, beginning with the most serious and continuing with the least. Some prefer to "soften the blow" on the confessor by beginning with the small sins first. The order in itself is of no importance, as long as the serious sins are, indeed, confessed.

Then we are ready to begin delineating our various sins. It is very important to give just enough information so the priest knows what you are talking about, but it is not good for either party to go into extreme or salacious details when the sins are against the sixth and ninth commandments. It is important to give some details concerning the others but not to take up too much time from the priest or the other penitents who may be waiting.

To make a good Confession, we should begin by making a proper examination of conscience beforehand. In the following pages an examination of conscience is given using the Ten Commandments as a guide.

Examination of Conscience
with the Ten Commandments

Prayer before the Examination of Conscience

Pray to the Holy Spirit to help you know yourself as He knows you and to be strong and sincere in your Confession without fear of human interests; that is, be concerned only about what God thinks. (Though He knows all you have ever done, He wants you to confess your sins within the confines of this great sacrament.) You can begin with the following prayer:

Come, Holy Spirit, fill the hearts of Your faithful and kindle in them the fire of Your love.

Send forth Your Spirit, and they shall be created. And You shall renew the face of the earth.

O God, who, by the light of the Holy Spirit, did instruct the hearts of the faithful, grant that by the

The Sacrament of Confession

same Holy Spirit, we may be truly wise and ever enjoy
His consolations.

Through the same Christ Our Lord. Amen.

Then you should consider the following:

- Have I ever made a bad Confession, deliberately omitting a mortal sin? *(We should not be so concerned with what a certain priest thinks of us, but rather, what Almighty God thinks.) A "bad Confession" is a mortal sin of sacrilege against this sacrament.*

- Have I failed to perform the penance given me? *If deliberate, then this invalidates the Confession as it is part of the "matter" of this sacrament.*

- Do I reverently and honestly examine my conscience before I enter the confessional? *It is a waste of the priest's time as well as the time of those who may be waiting in line if we go in and then start thinking about our sins. Before Confession is the time to think about our sins, not during or after.*

First Commandment

I AM THE LORD YOUR GOD: YOU SHALL NOT
HAVE STRANGE GODS BEFORE ME.

- Do I believe in God and love Him above all else?

- Have I worshipped or taken part in the worship of another deity?

- Have I left the Church and joined another religious group? *This is the sin of apostasy, which is mortal and demands that we return officially and make reparation, sometimes publicly, before being received back into full communion with the Church.*

- Have I taken part in devil worship and other superstitious practices that are contrary to God and His dignity? Have I been involved in the occult?

The Sacrament of Confession

- Do I consult horoscopes or other forms of divinization?

- Have I made a habit of going to services of a religion other than Catholic? *To do so would endanger our soul and make our Faith, the Mass, etc., seem to be the same as worship in an erroneous religion. It is a sin of syncretism.*

- Have I attended the attempted marriage of a Catholic outside the Church? *To do so is to commit an act of sacrilege and condone a mortal sin of another.*

- Do I belong to or support in any way any secret society (such as the Freemasons, Rosicrucians, etc.) that is against the Church? *Catholics who join these are automatically excommunicated.*[1]

- Do I know my Faith and seek always to continue to educate myself in it?

- Do I spend time reading non–Catholic religious literature or watching such movies and TV programs?

---

[1] Sacred Congregation for the Doctrine of Faith, "Declaration on Masonic Associations" (November 26, 1983).

- Do I read anti-Catholic literature?

- Do I pray every day and put God first in my life?

- Do I commend myself to God and His holy Will?

- Do I pray daily? Do I seek to attend Mass other than on Sundays and participate in all other devotions available to us in the Church for our own spiritual growth?

- Do I say the Rosary daily or often?

- Do I pray the Stations of the Cross at least on Fridays of Lent, if not more often?

- Have I been irreverent of God, our Lady, or the saints, as well as the sacraments and practices of the Faith?

- Do I make fun of or ridicule those who are faithful Catholics?

- Have I held the opinion of indifferentism—that all religions are the same?

- Have I presumed on the mercy of God? On His forgiveness?

The Sacrament of Confession

- Have I despaired? Have I thought that my sins are too much for even God to forgive?

- Have I hated God at any time?

- Do I put anyone or anything before God in my life?

Second Commandment

THOU SHALT NOT TAKE THE NAME OF
THE LORD THY GOD IN VAIN.

- Have I ever taken God's name in vain?

- Do I use the name of God or Jesus as a swear word?

- Do I use these names lightly and irreverently? (Such as the now common expression "OMG"?)

- Do I keep my promises to God?

- Have I been disrespectful or irreverent of any sacred person or thing?

- Have I cursed God or anyone in His name?

- Have I ever received a sacrament disrespectfully or sacrilegiously?

Third Commandment

REMEMBER TO KEEP HOLY THE
LORD'S DAY (THE SABBATH).

- Do I attend and seek to participate in the Holy Sacrifice of the Mass on Sundays and holy days of obligation?

- Am I often late for Mass?

- Do I ever leave Mass before it is over?

- Am I easily distracted, or do I daydream, during the Mass or sermon?

- Do I cause anyone else (e.g., children or elderly dependents) to miss Mass?

- Do I perform any unnecessary work on Sundays? *We should try to prepare ourselves the day before.*

The Sacrament of Confession

- Do I participate in any extra devotions (Benediction, Rosary, or Vespers) on Sundays? *These are there for my benefit—not God's.*

- Have I gone shopping on Sunday? *An emergency is an exception. We should do our grocery shopping on another day or night.*

- Have I been involved in commerce on Sunday?

- Do I use the extra rest time to visit the sick or shut-ins? Or elderly relatives and friends? Nursing homes? Prisoners—when that is possible or advisable?

- Do I use the time to read good spiritual books, the *Catechism of the Catholic Church*, or the lives of the saints?

- Do I teach my children the Faith? *Sunday is a perfect day for that.*

- Do I endanger my soul with unholy entertainments?

Fourth Commandment

- Do I love and respect my parents and guardians?

- Am I obedient to their orders?

- Do I show respect to those in authority?

- Do I show love and respect to my priest, my bishop, and the hierarchy?

- Am I respectful to elders?

- Am I respectful to my spouse and my children, and do I give good example?

- Do I take care of my parents' needs, if any?

The Sacrament of Confession

- Do I call and/or visit my parents frequently? Or those who helped raise me? Or any sick or elderly relatives and friends?

- Am I respectful to my teachers and professors?

- Are my children baptized in the Catholic Faith as soon as possible after birth?

- Do I neglect their Catholic upbringing?

- Do I take an active part in my children's religious instruction?

- Do I fail to advise my children if they are in error of the Faith or morals?

- Do I discipline them when needed?

- Have I been modest in front of them?

- Do I make sure they dress modestly?

- Have I argued with my spouse in front of them?

- Have I denied their freedom to marry or follow a religious vocation?

- Have I advised them about friends who are potentially a danger to their soul or body?

- Have I advised them when they are choosing a spouse for their future?

- Have I made sure that my children follow the precepts of the Church, especially regarding Mass, Confession, Holy Communion, Confirmation, and Holy Matrimony?

- Do I follow the prescriptions of the Church about burying the dead? *Though cremation is allowed, but not recommended, the ashes of the dead must be buried properly in a consecrated cemetery. It is never allowed to keep them as souvenirs, within the home, or to scatter them anywhere.*

Fifth Commandment

- Have I killed anyone?

- Have I hastened the death of anyone by administering or encouraging overmedicating with morphine or permitting euthanasia of those who are sick, elderly, or dying? *God knows well what each person needs to suffer, no matter how much, to keep them from the fires of Hell and assure their way into Purgatory, and later, Heaven. To shorten their lives could be very harmful to them. It is also playing God.*

- Have I had any part in a so-called therapeutic abortion?

- Did I pay for someone to have an abortion?

The Sacrament of Confession

- Did I facilitate someone having an abortion by driving that person to the place of abortion, for instance?

- Have I used any contraceptives?

- Have I made use of sterilization for myself or my spouse? If I have done so, have I tried to make amends and go to Confession as soon as possible? *Such usage makes a mockery out of the matrimonial act and prevents life.*

- Have I contemplated suicide? *Even our own life belongs only to God.*

- Have I assisted in anyone's attempt to commit suicide?

- Have I used my right to vote to promote the moral teachings of the Church in regard to life, sexuality, and the family?

- Have I voted for someone who is pro-abortion?

- Have I used violence or sought revenge on anyone? *Self-defense is exempted here as well as military service and the rightful defense of the nation.*

- Have I oppressed anyone?

- Have I forced anyone to act against his or her conscience?

- Have I hated anyone? Have I caused others to fight?

- Do I take pleasure at others' misfortunes?

- Have I mutilated my body? *Tattoos and piercings would traditionally violate this.*

- Do I misuse alcohol or drugs (legal or not)? *A good rule to follow regarding alcohol is not to have any over the amount at which it would be considered illegal to drive.*

- Do I eat, sleep, and exercise in a healthy way to take care of the temple of my body? *Moderation is the rule—neither too much nor too little.*

- Do I drive at excessive speeds—especially where there may be children, pedestrians, or animals? Do I drive too slowly and tempt others to impatience or even unsafe actions in driving?

- Do I use a cell phone for dialing and texting while driving? *While Bluetooth is available today, talking may still impede us from concentrating on safe driving.*

- Have I hurt, maimed, or killed an animal without necessity?

The Sacrament of Confession

- Do I respect the Lord's creation or misuse and waste it in any way?

- Do I waste water, food, electricity, fuel, or any of God's gifts?

- Do I thank God every day for my life, health, and all His gifts?

- Do I seek to love all and to share with those who are less fortunate than I?

Sixth and Ninth Commandments

THOU SHALT NOT COMMIT ADULTERY.

THOU SHALT NOT COVET (ENVY, DESIRE) THY NEIGHBOR'S WIFE.

- Have I been guilty of any impure action with myself or with another? Have I touched myself or another impurely? *Masturbation is a grave sin against our body and against purity and should always be confessed.*

- Have I looked at impure pictures, videos, or websites? *These are not only against the respect we owe others but also that which we owe our own bodies, which are temples of the Holy Spirit by Baptism and Confirmation.*

The Sacrament of Confession

- Have I engaged in any sexual activity outside of marriage? *This would be the mortal sin of fornication. Being engaged to someone does not give us the right to have sexual intimacy with that person. Sexual activity between engaged couples needs to be confessed.*

- If I am married, have I engaged in sexual activity with another person? *This would be the mortal sin of adultery.*

- Has every sexual act within marriage been open to the transmission of life? *Otherwise, it becomes the mortal sin of mutual masturbation. Sex is not only for pleasure but for the promotion of the human race and the Church.*

- Have I thought of others as sexual objects for my pleasure and enjoyment?

- Have I been guilty of homosexual activity? *The Bible and the Magisterium of the Church continually regard this as a serious sin against nature.*

- Have I been guilty of sodomy (anal sex) with my spouse or with any other person? *That is condemned by the Bible and the Magisterium of the Church.*

- Have I engaged in prolonged embraces which could result in temptation to me and the other person?

- Have I engaged in passionate kissing? *Our bodies tell us the whole story. Such kissing—often called "French"—arouses us sexually, and it may lead us to further and more serious sins against purity. They should be only for married spouses.*

- Have I engaged in premarital sexual activity? *It is not only a sin against purity but also against Holy Matrimony.*

- Have I been an occasion of sin to another person? *This includes the way we dress, the way we look at someone, and the way we touch someone.*

- Have I used indecent language? Did I listen to it out of curiosity or sexual desire?

- Have I boasted of my past sins—of my "conquests"?

- Do I keep bad company? *Many times, especially in youth, the sins that people commit are because of fear of being ridiculed by those with whom we keep company. We should always strive to make friends and surround ourselves with those we know to be good Catholics with good morals.*

- Do I control my imagination? *In the Confiteor, we ask forgiveness for sins of thought. Thoughts, then, can be sins and even mortal sins if we indulge in them and draw enjoyment from them.*

- Do I pray and perform penances to try to avoid temptation and sin?

- Do I avoid laziness, gluttony, idleness, and excessive recreation that could lead to temptation against purity? *St. Thomas taught that gluttony and excessive use of alcohol can lead to other sins of passion — including impurity.*

- Do I frequent dances, parties, and other forms of entertainment that can lead me to sins against purity?

- Have I been alone with someone who may be an occasion of sin?

- Do I think of the immortal and perishable souls of those with whom I may commit or have committed sins against purity? Do I try to lead them to repentance and Confession? *I am my neighbor's keeper here, too.*

- Have I desired another person's wife or husband? Fiancée?

With regard to these and all sins, we should not be embarrassed to tell the priest in Confession what we have done. He has heard it all before. You will not shock him. Furthermore, he is concerned with your salvation and wants to help you—not to condemn you. Confessors are advised to be kind and gentle, even when firm in maintaining the truth of the moral Magisterium of God and His Church.

Seventh and Tenth Commandments

THOU SHALT NOT STEAL.

THOU SHALT NOT COVET (ENVY, DESIRE)
THY NEIGHBOR'S GOODS.

With the Seventh and Tenth Commandments, there is a very important warning that must be made clear and understood. If one steals anything from anyone or destroys their reputation, one cannot be forgiven until one makes restitution. (If this is impossible, then some other means acceptable to the parties, or if the victim is dead and has no heirs, acceptable to the confessor must be found.)

- Have I stolen anything? (What and how much?)

- Have I borrowed any money from anyone while knowing that I could not repay it? *This is tantamount to both a lie and a theft.*

The Sacrament of Confession

- Have I neglected or refused to pay debts?

- Have I returned things I borrowed?

- Have I damaged the property of others—deliberately, carelessly, or negligently—and failed to make restitution?

- Have I cheated others in any way? *This includes games, sports, as well as school.*

- Have I cheated my employer of an honest day's work—such as by daydreaming, talking or texting unnecessarily, playing games, or browsing the Internet?

- When having the means, have I refused to help others in authentic need? *This does not include panhandlers or those who beg with no real need. That involves a whole other treatise. If they refuse to work, then they are also stealing from those from whom they beg. Our society and the Church have many means to lawfully and authentically help those in need.*

- Have I been generous with those truly poor? *This includes relatives as well as friends, or, for instance, other members of our Church or parish.*

- Have I been careful to pay the tithe to the Lord by giving my first 10 percent to my parish? To other Catholic institutions?

- Do I work (study) diligently and use my time wisely?

- Am I jealous or envious of the possessions of others? *To covet also implies that I would go to an extent to have what belongs to them, including theft or robbery.*

- Am I greedy?

- Am I selfish?

- Do I live for my material possessions and not lay up treasure in Heaven for myself?

- Do I put my trust in God and His Divine Providence that He will take care of all my needs?

Eighth Commandment

- Have I lied about anyone—thus committing the mortal sin of calumny?

- Have I caused anyone harm by lying?

- Have I rashly judged others? *If I am not privy to all the facts, then I should not judge on the guilt of anyone. It is always better to assume innocence.*

- Have I broken someone's confidence, thus causing embarrassment, or even harm, to anyone? *Even if something is true, that does not give us the freedom to reveal their private affairs to anyone else.*

The Sacrament of Confession

- Am I critical of others in my thoughts? Or in my words?

- Do I gossip about others? *Just as none of us likes to be the object of gossip, we also should avoid it regarding others. In Spanish, there is a saying: "When you see your neighbor's beard on fire, put yours in the water."*

- Do I encourage others to gossip with me about others by "lending" them an ear, i.e., an opportunity?

- Have I perjured myself? *This is to make a false oath. Perjury under the name of God as a guarantee is also a sin against the Second Commandment.*

- Have I flattered others (dishonestly)? *For example: "You are the best singer" or "You are my dearest friend." And so on ...*

- Am I sincere in my dealings with others? Or am I a hypocrite?

Prayer after the Examination of Conscience

O my God, I cry unto Thee with the prodigal: Father, I have sinned against Heaven and before Thee; I am no longer worthy to be called Thy son. I have gone astray like a sheep that is lost. O seek Thy servant, for I have not forgotten Thy Commandments. Enter not into judgment with Thy servant, O Lord. Spare me for Thy mercy's sake. Prove me, O God, and know my heart; examine me, and know my paths. Thou Whose property is always to have mercy and to spare, O meet me in pity, embrace me in love, and forgive me all my sin. I confess my sins unto Thee, O Christ, Healer of our souls, O Lord of Life. Heal me, heal me of my spiritual sickness, Thou Who art long-suffering and of tender mercy; heal me, O Lord Christ. Accept my supplications, O Thou Holy Spirit, unto Whom every heart is open, every desire known, and from Whom no secret is hid, and Who givest life to our souls; hear and answer, O Spirit of God. O Heavenly Father, Who willest not that any sinner should perish, give me true repentance for this my sin, that I perish not! To what misery am I come by my own fault! O merciful God, pity and forgive me for Jesus' sake. Thine eyes, O God, are as a flame of fire searching my inmost heart. O pardon my sin, for it is great! Thou, God, seest me in all the foulness of my sins! Blessed Jesus, speak for me, plead for me, come between my soul and my offended God, that I perish not. Amen.[2]

[2] From *A Manual of Prayers for the Use of the Catholic Laity* (New York: Christian Press Association Publishing Company, 1896), 282.

Other Confession Prayers

Acts of Contrition

Outside the Confessional

O my God, I am heartily sorry for having offended Thee, and I detest all my sins because of Thy just punishments (or: because I dread the loss of Heaven and the pains of Hell), but most of all because they offend Thee, my God, Who art all good and deserving of all my love. I firmly resolve, with the help of Thy grace, to confess my sins, to do penance, and to amend my life. Amen.

Inside the Confessional, before Absolution

O my God, I am heartily sorry for having offended Thee, and I detest all my sins because of Thy just punishments (or: because I dread the loss of Heaven and the pains of Hell), but most of all because they offend Thee, my God, Who art all good and deserving of all my love. I firmly resolve with the help of Thy grace to sin no more, to amend my life, and to avoid the near occasion of sin. Amen.

Psalm 51

The Psalms, especially the Miserere (Ps. 51), can be used as preparation before and reparation after Confession.

Miserere

Have mercy on me, God, in accord with
    your merciful love;
in your abundant compassion blot out my
    transgressions.
Thoroughly wash away my guilt;
and from my sin cleanse me.
For I know my transgressions;
my sin is always before me.
Against you, you alone have I sinned;
I have done what is evil in your eyes
So that you are just in your word,

The Sacrament of Confession

and without reproach in your judgment.
Behold, I was born in guilt,
in sin my mother conceived me.
Behold, you desire true sincerity;
and secretly you teach me wisdom.
Cleanse me with hyssop, that I may be pure;
wash me, and I will be whiter than snow.
You will let me hear gladness and joy;
the bones you have crushed will rejoice.

Turn away your face from my sins;
blot out all my iniquities.
A clean heart create for me, God;
renew within me a steadfast spirit.
Do not drive me from before your face,
nor take from me your holy spirit.
Restore to me the gladness of your salvation;
uphold me with a willing spirit.
I will teach the wicked your ways,
that sinners may return to you.
Rescue me from violent bloodshed, God,
    my saving God,
and my tongue will sing joyfully of your justice.
Lord, you will open my lips;
and my mouth will proclaim your praise.

For you do not desire sacrifice or I would give it;
a burnt offering you would not accept.
My sacrifice, O God, is a contrite spirit;
a contrite, humbled heart, O God, you will
    not scorn.

Treat Zion kindly according to your good will;
build up the walls of Jerusalem.
Then you will desire the sacrifices of the just,
burnt offering and whole offerings;
then they will offer up young bulls on your altar.

The Catechism on the Sacrament of Confession

Catechism of Trent

(Section on Penance)

"It cannot, therefore, be a matter of surprise that the enemy of the human race, in his efforts to destroy utterly the Catholic Church, should through the agency of the ministers of his wicked designs, have assailed with all his might this bulwark, as it were, of Christian virtue. It should be shown, therefore, that the institution of Confession is most useful and even necessary to us."[3] The Catechism goes on to explain how this powerful sacrament can erase such and so many crimes. It is instituted by Christ Himself: "After His Resurrection [the very first Easter Sunday]

---

[3] *Catechism of the Council of Trent for Parish Priests,* trans. Robert A. McHugh, O.P. (New York: Joseph F. Wagner, 1947), 281.

He breathed on the Apostles, assembled together, saying: 'Receive ye the Holy Ghost, whose sins you shall forgive, they shall be forgiven; and whose sins you shall retain, they are retained.'"[4]

"Not only are the faithful to be taught that Confession was instituted by our Lord. They are to be reminded that, by authority of the Church, certain rites and solemn ceremonies have been added."[5] Thus, there is a formula which the Church commands for the validity of the sacrament (as with all other sacraments). These require the words, regardless of any others: "May Our Lord, Jesus Christ, absolve you, and [by His Authority] I absolve you from your sins. In the Name of the Father, and of the Son, and of the Holy Spirit. Amen." This is the "form" of this sacrament. The "matter" or "elements" of the sacrament are sins confessed and the satisfaction rendered afterward. Thus, if we are absolved and do not perform our penance given by the priest, we are not absolved (with the exception of intention to perform it which is interrupted by an accident or serious illness, resulting in death). Unintentionally forgetting our penance can be a mitigating factor, but it should be of more importance to us.

4 Ibid., 284.
5 Ibid., 285.

"Confession, then, is defined: *A Sacramental accusation of one's sins, made to obtain pardon by virtue of the keys.*"[6] (That is, the keys given to the Church in the person of Saint Peter, see Matt. 16:19.) As such, Confession should be made often. It must be entire, omitting nothing deliberately. If a person deliberately omits any sins, especially mortal, then the Confession is invalid or null. Not only will the person have to go to Confession again, but he/she must also confess that the sin of sacrilege, omitting sins deliberately, has been committed at the previous Confession.[7] If any sin is forgotten, it will be forgiven. There is no need to repeat the entire Confession. However, the penitent should, at the next occasion, mention that a particular serious sin was forgotten (thus the necessity for a thorough examination of conscience before each Confession.) Confession must be made in private—before the priest. It must be prudent, modest, and brief.[8]

The next important element of Confession is satisfaction for our sins. In the first instance, this satisfaction depends on whatever the confessor has determined to be salutary for the penitent. Both extremes are to be avoided.

[6] Ibid., 283.
[7] Ibid., 289.
[8] Ibid., 289–290.

The Sacrament of Confession

A confessor should not just give such light penances that it becomes almost a mockery of the sacrament or of the seriousness of sin. On the other hand, he should not demand such a severe penance that the penitent goes away dejected or angry and commits another sin by refusing to perform the penance. It is always better to err on the side of mercy. The confessor will oftentimes, in order not to discourage a penitent, perform some or most of the penance himself. (After all, is that not that which Christ did in His Passion and death on the Cross?) In truth, not all the penances in the world can offer proper satisfaction to God for any of our offenses. The one exception is that of the necessity of restitution of goods stolen or damaged, and of the good name or reputation of someone whom we have slandered or calumniated. "No person is to be absolved until he has first faithfully promised to restore all that belongs to others."[9]

So satisfaction and penance on our part is not only important, it is essential for us to be forgiven from our sins, for the absolution of the priest at the sacrament to fully take effect. Again, the first regards that penance given to us by the confessor. In addition, each of us must perform penances all throughout our lives for our own past sins as well

[9] Ibid, 304.

as the sins of those who have not yet repented. This involves charity, first to Almighty God Who has been offended by our sins, and all sins, and then to our fellow brethren who have need of us.[10]

[10] Ibid, 304–306.

Catechism of the Catholic Church

(ARTICLES 1420–1498)

Citing the Dogmatic Constitution on the Church, *Lumen Gentium* (11.2) the *Catechism* says: "Those who approach the Sacrament of Penance obtain pardon from God's mercy for the offense committed against Him, and are, at the same time, reconciled with the Church which they have wounded by their sins and which by charity, by example, and by prayer labors for their conversion" (CCC 1492). In a very detailed exposition to which you can refer yourself as we have pointed out above, the *Catechism* delves into this marvelous sacrament more than any other before it. In addition, there is a very comprehensive section in this *Catechism* that goes into the Commandments, the precepts of the Church, and other founts from which we can obtain knowledge of both the way of perfection, as well as the many ways in which we can offend God, the Church and our neighbor, and therefore, for which we need to obtain pardon (CCC 2032–2557). Thus, "the Church, the 'pillar and bulwark of the Truth,' has received this solemn command of Christ from the Apostles to announce the saving Truth. To the Church belongs the right always and everywhere to announce the principles, including those pertaining to the social order, and to make judgments on any human affairs to the extent that they are required by the fundamental rights of the human person or the salvation of souls" (CCC 2032).

In this light, by the Gift of the instructions of the Holy Spirit promised to the Church and the apostles by Our Lord before He ascended into Heaven until the end of time (Matt. 28:20), we can now look at some of the principles by which we can both live a truly Christian life and learn how to avoid offending God and each other.

Guiding Principles for Your Confession

Below we give not only the Ten Commandments and precepts of the Church, but also the Corporal and Spiritual Works of Mercy, as well as the four cardinal virtues. All of these will assist us in making a habitual and thorough examination of conscience. It is important to seek to grow spiritually always. One should find the best confessor possible in the area or nearby and go to him regularly. St. John XXIII, and many other saints, always recommended that we should choose the "best" possible confessor — not the easiest to get along with or most lenient. It is better to have a strict confessor in this life and end it well, prepared for eternity, than to come upon a negative judgment from the Almighty.

The Precepts of the Church

1. You shall attend Mass on Sundays and on holy days of obligation.
2. You shall confess your sins at least once a year.
3. You shall humbly receive your Creator in Holy Communion at least during the Easter season.
4. You shall keep holy (i.e., sanctify) the holy days of obligation.
5. You shall observe prescribed days of fasting and abstinence.
6. You have the duty of providing for the material needs of the Church (namely your parish) according to your means (the tithe).
7. You shall observe the laws of Holy Mother Church concerning the Holy Sacrament of Matrimony.

The Decalogue — Ten Commandments

1. I am the Lord thy God: thou shalt not have strange gods before Me.
2. Thou shalt not take the Name of the Lord thy God in vain.
3. Remember to keep holy the Lord's Day (the Sabbath).
4. Thou shalt honor thy father and thy mother.
5. Thou shalt not kill.
6. Thou shalt not commit adultery.
7. Thou shalt not steal.
8. Thou shalt not bear false witness against thy neighbor.
9. Thou shalt not covet (envy, desire) thy neighbor's wife.
10. Thou shalt not covet (envy, desire) thy neighbor's goods.

The Seven Spiritual Works of Mercy

1. To admonish the sinner.
2. To instruct the ignorant.
3. To counsel the doubtful.
4. To comfort the sorrowful.
5. To bear wrongs patiently.
6. To forgive all injuries.
7. To pray for the living and for the dead.

The Seven Corporal Works of Mercy

1. To feed the hungry.
2. To give drink to the thirsty.
3. To clothe the naked.
4. To visit the imprisoned.
5. To shelter the homeless.
6. To visit the sick.
7. To bury the dead.

The Beatitudes

1. Blessed are the poor in spirit, for theirs is the Kingdom of Heaven.
2. Blessed are the meek, for they shall possess the earth.
3. Blessed are they who mourn, for they shall be comforted.
4. Blessed are they who hunger and thirst for justice, for they shall be satisfied.
5. Blessed are the merciful, for they shall obtain mercy.
6. Blessed are the pure of heart, for they shall see God.
7. Blessed are the peacemakers, for they shall be called children of God.
8. Blessed are they who suffer persecution for justice's sake, for theirs is the Kingdom of Heaven.

The Beatitudes contain, in substance, the Law of God and all the evangelical counsels of perfection.

The Theological Virtues

Faith, hope, and charity—*They are theological because they have God as their principal objects. "They touch God."*

The Moral or Cardinal Virtues

Prudence, justice, fortitude, and temperance—*They are cardinal because the whole spiritual life hinges on them.*

In addition: filial piety, patriotism, obedience, veracity, patience, religion, humility, chastity, liberality, meekness, abstinence, zeal, and brotherly love.

Bibliography

Arrieta, Juan Ignatio, ed. *Code of Canon Law: Fourth Edition.* South Bend, IN: Midwest Theological Forum, 2022.

Catechism of the Catholic Church. Washington, D.C.: United States Conference of Catholic Bishops, 2001.

Halligan, Father Nicholas, O.P. *The Ministry of the Celebration of the Sacraments, Volume 2: Sacraments of Reconciliation.* New York: Society of St. Paul, 1973.

Kane, Father John A. *How to Make a Good Confession.* Manchester, New Hampshire: Sophia Institute Press, 2001.

Miller, Father Frederick L., S.T.D. *A Primer for Confession.* New Hope, KY: St. Martin de Porres, 1989.

Morrow, Louis LaRavoire, S.T.D. *My Catholic Faith.* St. Marys, Kansas: Sarto House, 2001.

New American Bible, revised edition. Washington, D.C.: Confraternity of Christian Doctrine, 2010.

Ripley, Canon Francis. *This Is the Catholic Faith: A Complete Explanation of the Catholic Faith.* Rockford, IL: TAN Books, 1999.

Third Plenary Council of Baltimore, *A Manual of Prayers: For the Use of the Catholic Laity.* Baltimore: Forgotten Books, 2017.

About the Author

The Very Reverend Canon Héctor R. G. Pérez y Robles is a priest of the Diocese of Pensacola-Tallahassee. He is the censor librorum and theologian for the diocese and serves as spiritual director of the Pensacola Comitium of the Legion of Mary. He is a canon and chaplain of the Military and Hospitaller Order of St. Lazarus of Jerusalem. He is a contributor to Our Sunday Visitor's *Catholic Encyclopedia* and has written many sermons and homilies, including "Three Days That Changed the World," available through Lighthouse Media.

Sophia Institute

Sophia Institute is a nonprofit institution that seeks to nurture the spiritual, moral, and cultural life of souls and to spread the gospel of Christ in conformity with the authentic teachings of the Roman Catholic Church.

Sophia Institute Press fulfills this mission by offering translations, reprints, and new publications that afford readers a rich source of the enduring wisdom of mankind.

Sophia Institute also operates the popular online resource CatholicExchange.com. *Catholic Exchange* provides world news from a Catholic perspective as well as daily devotionals and articles that will help readers to grow in holiness and live a life consistent with the teachings of the Church.

In 2013, Sophia Institute launched Sophia Institute for Teachers to renew and rebuild Catholic culture through service to Catholic education. With the goal of nurturing the spiritual, moral, and cultural life of souls, and an abiding respect for the role and work of teachers, we strive to provide materials and programs that are at once enlightening to the mind and ennobling to the heart; faithful and complete, as well as useful and practical.

Sophia Institute gratefully recognizes the Solidarity Association for preserving and encouraging the growth of our apostolate over the course of many years. Without their generous and timely support, this book would not be in your hands.

www.SophiaInstitute.com
www.CatholicExchange.com
www.SophiaInstituteforTeachers.org